To: Kaye, as always

Edited by: Vreni Merriam and Marsha Weese

Copyright © 2013 by John Merriam

Published by University Book Store Press
Printed on the Espresso Book Machine
4326 University Way NE
Seattle, WA 98105
www.ubookstore.com

ISBN: 978-1-937358-36-5

BUSTED

(Why I Became a Lawyer)

by John Merriam

It was 1973 and I was down on my luck. My girlfriend Laura had moved out and taken her kids back to California. Without her share of the rent, I couldn't afford our house in the Magnolia district of Seattle and had to stay with friends, sleeping on couches. By September I was broke and sick with a bad cold. The only good thing going on in my life was that I didn't have to worry about being drafted and sent to Viet Nam.

Earlier, in 1970, I'd joined the merchant marine to get a draft deferment. Thirteen days after I got my seamen's papers, President Nixon repealed the deferment for merchant seamen. My birth date drew #68 in the second draft lottery later that year, which meant I was going to be inducted into the army pronto, so I immediately applied for admission to the University of Washington to get a student deferment. I stayed in the merchant marine, catching ships during every vacation for the money to stay in school. I didn't do very well at the UW, unable to force myself to study, and lost my deferment due to low grades. As luck would have it, during my Pre-Induction Physical exam I was given a 4F deferment for flat feet -- the way that happened is a story all by itself.

As soon as I beat the draft, I caught a ship for the first three months of 1972 and came back with my pockets jingling. It was shortly after that when I moved in with Laura and her kids. I tried to make a go of it with my girlfriend and didn't ship out for over a year, but it didn't work

1

out. I took UW classes during that time -- more out of boredom than anything else -- and did better without the draft hanging over my head. For money, I got by on unemployment and working odd jobs under the table. But those opportunities dried up and there was no more money to live on, to say nothing of paying tuition. I knew it was time to catch a ship.

I

The war was winding down and shipping wasn't as good as it had been, but on September 25, 1973 several positions aboard the S.S. Summit were posted on the job board. The Summit was a Sea-Land ship that ran up and down the Aleutian Island chain in Alaska. She had a hard time keeping a full crew during the winter months because the weather was so miserable. It looked like a lot of seamen decided that summer was over and were getting off.

At the time I held a B-book -- second-tier seniority -- in the Seafarers International Union. The SIU hiring hall in Seattle was at 1st and Wall. Competitive bidding occurred every hour during job calls, but no B-books were getting out. To keep my B seniority I had to get 90 days of sea-time every year. If I didn't catch a ship by October 2nd and stay on until the end of the year I would be reduced to a C-card starting in 1974, which would effectively end my job prospects in the merchant marine. That gave me one more reason to be depressed.

The union Patrolman called out the jobs at the top of the hour. Bidding for available billets on the Summit was spirited until he called for a Wiper. Wiper is a hard, dirty job -- the lowest rating in the engine department. No A-books threw in their registration cards and I got it.

The next morning I boarded the S.S. Summit at Pier 5 on Harbor Island at the mouth of the Duwamish River. She was a T-2 tanker, built at the end of World War II, that had been converted into a freighter. About 600 feet in length and displacing 10,000 tons of water, the Summit had been turned into one of the original containerships by Sea-Land, the company that introduced the concept of containerized cargo. She carried a crew of 11 licensed officers and 28 unlicensed seamen. Thirty-five-foot containers, many of them refrigerated, filled the cargo holds and were stacked three-high on deck. Toward the stern, the stacks were interrupted by the "house"-- a superstructure higher than the containers and topped by the bridge, with radar and other conning equipment -- for navigation and communication -- rising higher yet.

S.S. stands for steamship. I'd sailed as Wiper once before and knew a little bit about engine rooms. I was soon to learn that the S.S. Summit was not a true steamship. Even though she burned oil to create steam, the steam on the Summit was used exclusively to spin turbines in generators rather than to turn the propeller shaft directly. Propulsion came from electricity produced by the generators, not from steam. The Summit was properly called a turbo-electric ship.

I was also soon to learn that Seattle was not part of the Summit's regular run. Usually staying up north, she was in Seattle for shipyard work. Constant beating in the punishing Alaskan waters resulted in trips south for repairs every couple months on average. Those trips also allowed the Summit to bring containers directly to Seattle, cargo that otherwise would have been dropped off in Kodiak, to be picked up by other Sea-Land containerships on a regular run between Seattle, Anchorage, and Kodiak.

I went to look for my new digs. Below the main deck I located a fo'c'sle marked for two Wipers. I opened the door and peered into an eight-by-ten-foot enclosure with a double bunk, two lockers, small desk, sink, and one porthole.

"Hey, man. Are you the new Wiper?"

I turned around and saw a skinny guy in his early 20s, a couple inches taller than me. He had long, frizzy red hair, styled like an Afro, and a trace of fading freckles. "Yeah, I'm John."

"I'm the Bull Wiper. Name's Pat. You've got the top bunk. After you stow your gear I'll show you the jobs you've got." He offered his hand at a 45-degree angle, rather than straight-on for a traditional handshake. I knew that 'Bull' Wiper was code for giving the other guy the worst jobs, but I didn't care. I was happy to be working. More importantly, Pat and I were about the same age and both of us had long hair. Hair was something of a badge during those polarized times, and the fact that we both wore it long made us instant allies. I grasped Pat's hand in the manner considered hip by 'those in the know.' "A couple of the Ordinaries are cool," Pat continued, referring to Ordinary Seamen, "but mostly there are drunken old farts on here. The guys from Seattle won't mess with you, but some leftovers who brought the ship around from New York are real assholes."

After I dumped out my duffel bag, Pat gave me a tour of the engine room. We started by descending a ladder, really a steep staircase, near the stern that went to the steering gear -- an electrically-powered device the size of a Buick that moved the rudder. Pat explained that the steering gear needed regular lubrication and was a good place to goof off because the Engineers rarely went there. From the steering gear we went down another ladder to the machine shop. I saw a huge metal lathe, work benches, a slew of tools, and storage bins for items such as nuts, bolts, etc. "This is where you'll spend a lot of your time," Pat said. "I'll show you the shaft alley later." He was referring to the narrow area between the engine room and the stern containing a large shaft from the engine that turned the propeller.

"Chief Kruger knows what he's doing," he continued. "But the watch Engineers are all idiots. The First (Assistant Engineer) is new and I haven't figured out his trip yet -- you'll be working a lot with him. I help the Chief with repairs on deck. You'll have to make sure the other Engineers have the right tools when they make repairs down here."

Pat led me from the machine shop to the fireroom, a dark, cramped space with two furnaces -- each as big as a cheap hotel room -- underneath two huge boilers. The Fireman was staring vacantly at the steam pressure gauges. "That's Arne," Pat whispered. "He won the contest for jacking-off the most times in one watch."

The main engine room was next to the fireroom. It was open and spacious with a ceiling up to the level of the main deck. Large steam pipes went to three generators. A long, eight-foot-high electrical panel stood next to the log desk, where an Oiler and a Third Assistant Engineer loitered looking very bored. "After you blow tubes," Pat told me, "you've got to hang out here so the First can see you. Make it look like you're busy. Sweep, mop, take out the garbage -- anything to pretend you're working."

After that, Pat took me to the bow to look at the 60-ton Manitowoc crane that he said was never used. "Sea-Land has a contract from the Navy to bring supplies to Adak near the end of the Aleutians. Part of the contract is that we've got to carry this crane in case we have to work cargo that can't be handled by the ship's gear in an emergency." The Summit had a gantry, her own crane, on two legs that straddled the ship, to move containers onto and off docks. "Sea-Land gets its operating costs plus a 10% profit from the Navy. That means you can put anything you want on your overtime sheet. The more money we get the more 10% gravy the company gets. The Chief will sign off on OT as long as you don't get outrageous. I work every night after supper from 1730 to 1945 (5:30 to 7:45 p.m.) and write 2200 (10:00 p.m.) on the OT sheet. Chief Kruger always signs it. He knows I'm a good worker." On the way back to the house, we saw a short AB (Able Seaman) walking toward us, holding a needle gun for chipping rust. The AB was almost as wide as he was tall. "Hey man," Pat said when the AB was close, "what's a short little fat fucker like you up to today?" If looks could kill, Pat would have died on the spot.

"Him and some of the other deck apes call me a 'hippie' and generally give me shit," Pat told me as we returned to our fo'c'sle. "Everybody on here is a misfit and people who live in glass houses shouldn't throw stones. There's only one reason to come to Alaska, and that's to make money. Anybody who talks about 'the romance of the sea' is full of shit. All the ABs are fucked-up alcoholics. They'd get fired on any other ship. The Shipping Articles say "no grog" -- this ship is supposed to be alcohol-free. The Bo's'n (deck boss), Frenchie, has Budweiser brought aboard by the pallet so he and the Electrician can stay drunk all the time. I don't mess with them and they don't mess with me."

The Summit left Pier 5 that afternoon and headed to Alaska at 16 knots -- about 19 miles-per-hour in land speed -- bound for Dutch Harbor.

"Why do they call it Dutch Harbor?" I asked Pat at breakfast the next day.

"I don't know. Some say that a Dutch ship put in there but I think that's bullshit. The Russians got to the Aleutians first and really fucked up those islands. They killed all the seals, cut down all the trees, and gave the natives alcohol. After America bought Alaska 100 years ago, the only difference is that Aleuts now get drunk on bourbon instead of vodka."

"How long does it take to get there?"

"Usually five or six days unless we hit a storm," he said.

"Where do we go after Dutch Harbor?" I asked as I finished up my eggs and bacon.

"Probably Kodiak. That's the only good port on this run. Something like 19 bars are there so all the alkies on here go crazy. There's dancing at some of the bars, and some of the taxi drivers are chicks. If you tip well and they like you, some of the drivers will go dancing and, if you're lucky, more than that."

"What are the other ports?" I asked.

"The only regular ports that we hit every run are Kodiak, Adak, Cordova, and Dutch Harbor. Cordova is as far east as we go. It's just a fishing town and not much is there but it's beautiful country. Prince William Sound is like Puget Sound must have looked with bigger mountains before white people fucked it up.

Bering Sea

Beaufort Sea

Alaska

Adak

Dillingham
Naknek

Dutch Harbor • Akutan
Sand Point
Kodiak
Homer
Seward • Cordova

North Pacific Ocean

Yukon Territory

Yakutat

Juneau
Sitka   B.C.
Petersburg
Wrangell
Ketchikan

Rest of Alaska | Southeast Alaska

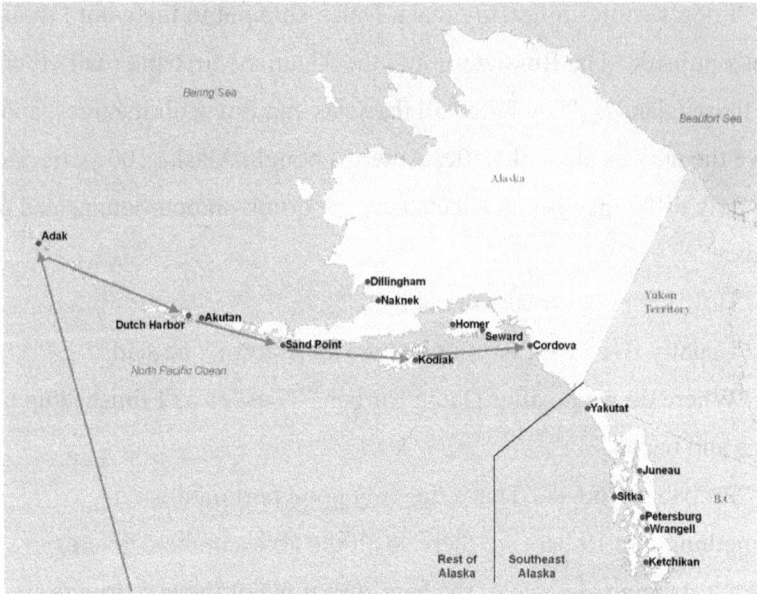

Route of S.S. Summit after leaving Seattle on 9/26/73

"At the other end is Adak," Pat continued. I listened willingly as he provided information. "That's as far out as we go on the Aleutian Chain, almost to the dateline and Russia. It's in the middle of nowhere and has a big Navy base with a lot of Marines. The Marines don't have anything to do except lift weights and sit around in the enlisted men's club drinking beer. They twist each other's ears for kicks. We get privileges at the base and can go to the service clubs for drinks. It's where the guys on here get cheap booze, at the base Exchange. The round-trip between Adak visits is 12 to 14 days so they've got to stock up. Everybody on that island is stir-crazy. The ratio of men to women in Alaska is 17-to-1; on Adak it's 100-to-1. I stay on the ship when we're there. The last time I went to a club on Adak I got in a fistfight with some Marine asshole. I won the fight but I had to outrun all his buddies to get back to the ship. They don't like merchant seamen to begin with because we make more money than they do. When Marines see long hair they start foaming at the mouth."

It was getting close to 0800, when we were supposed to go to work, but Pat seemed in no hurry so I asked another question. "What's in the containers?"

"Toothpaste, hot dogs, and a lot of alcohol, basically. We bring supplies to all the Aleutian Islands and Cordova and pick up containers of fish and crab to bring to Kodiak. There're stops in a lot of little shit-ass fishing villages along the way. Most days we tie up at least once at some island for a little while. That breaks the monotony, but there's no reason to go ashore. Like Sand Point for example, just before the start of the Aleutians, where we stop a lot: there's nothing there except a cannery with a bunch of Filipinos processing fish -- they don't even have a bar! I'd make a play for some of the cute chicks from Manila on the processing line, but they're married and those Filipinos all carry knives.

"Hey, it's 0759!" Pat got up. "The new First is a stickler about punctuality. Let's go below. I'm Bull Wiper so you've got to blow tubes. C'mon, I'll show you."

Pat showed me in what order to pull a series of chains attached to the ends of the two furnaces, at the top just beneath the boilers. The chains rotated wheels that shot superheated steam, in sequence, onto the outside of copper water tubes that went from the boilers into the furnaces. Blowing tubes means to 'blow' soot off the 'tubes' of water in the furnaces so that the water in the boilers could be heated more efficiently. It was hard work. When I finished 20 minutes later my arms hurt, I was out of breath, and felt weak and feverish. 'This will be a hell of a way to wake up every morning,' I thought.

"Don't worry," Pat said, looking at me with a combination of pity and disgust. "This job will toughen you up quick."

Steaming to Dutch Harbor, I settled in to my duties as Wiper. The regular work hours were from 0800 to 1700, with lunch from 1200 to 1300 and 15-minute coffee breaks at 1000 and 1500. By unwritten rule in the Summit's Engine Department, everybody knocked off at 1130 for lunch and 15 minutes early for the coffee breaks. After blowing tubes, no day was the same for me. I often helped the First with repairs in the engine room and shaft alley, fixing pumps and grinding valves while Pat did repairs on deck with Chief Kruger. There was always a lot to do in the machine shop because none of the Engineers was very good about putting away tools. And there was trash to dump over the side -- I was told that, once we were more than three miles off shore, it was legal to dump anything into the ocean. When nothing else was going on I swept, mopped, or as my rating suggested, wiped up oil.

Supper was from 1700-1800 but we always knocked off early at 1630. Work after 1800 was overtime, if we wanted it, and both Pat and I did. "I do easy jobs after dinner," Pat explained while we stood in the shaft alley at 1730, "like painting. Tonight we're going to paint International Orange on the lines for compressed air. Pat pointed up to a maze of brass and iron piping that looked to me like leftovers on a plate of spaghetti.

"OK," I said, "which ones are the lines for compressed air?"

"You've got to trace them from the air compressors. My project is to color code every line in the engine room: black for fuel oil, yellow for lube oil, silver for steam lines and white for water involved in the steam cycle, green for sanitary (sewer) water, blue for drinking water, and red for seawater to the fire pumps. This will be gravy overtime for months! Chief Kruger loves my idea. He says it will help his incompetent Engineers do their job."

Pat and I spread orange paint, working quickly until coffee-time that evening, 1945 hours, when we knocked off for good. We both wrote down 2200 on our OT sheets as our quitting time.

The work week was seven days, the same every day. The difference on Saturdays, Sundays and holidays was that we got paid a higher, premium rate of overtime for every hour worked -- 12 hours per day (theoretically) in my case. I didn't need an abacus to realize that I would be grossing at least $1200 per month -- by far the most money I'd ever earned!

II

My head was still spinning from the amount of money I was making when we tied up at Dutch Harbor. I worked overtime after supper instead of going ashore. Pat told me that Dutch was a good-for-nothing port with one bar and not much else. 'I'll check it out next time,' I thought, while on my way to find fresh paintbrushes. All I saw of Unalaska, the island on which Dutch Harbor was located, was a hilly landscape -- bleak, barren and windswept. Technically, I learned later, Dutch Harbor is on Amaknak Island and connected to the island and town of Unalaska by a bridge.

From Dutch we steamed to Adak by way of the Bering Sea, traversing along the north side of the Aleutians. Leaning on the rail I saw maybe a dozen islands of volcanic rock and little else. Gray clouds and the sea seemed to converge well before the horizon and I got a hint of the winter to come.

It was an unusually clear day when we arrived in Adak. During the morning coffee break, I came up on deck to look around. Adak looked flatter and even more desolate than Unalaska, if that was possible. I watched two otters frolicking around pilings at the pier we were tied to. The Chief Steward, Paul, was standing on the fantail, throwing chunks of raw meat into the water for a couple of brown-feathered eagles. The huge birds would swoop over the water and deftly grab their hors d'oeuvres. The eagles appeared young, without full coloring, and I couldn't tell if they were golden or bald. About 40 seagulls were flying around, squawking loudly but careful to keep their distance, insanely jealous that the eagles were getting all the good stuff. After I watched them snatch several offerings, the eagles seemed to grow bored with this sport. They stayed perched on a telephone pole after the Steward threw another chunk of raw meat over the side. A seagull got brave, dove toward the slowly-sinking beef, and plucked it from just beneath the surface. As the seagull struggled to regain altitude, the two eagles swooped down flying in formation. The first eagle snatched the meat out of the seagull's mouth. The second eagle crossed in front of the seagull's throat with an extended talon. The seagull went into a bloody tailspin and splashed into the harbor.

I didn't go ashore that time in Adak.

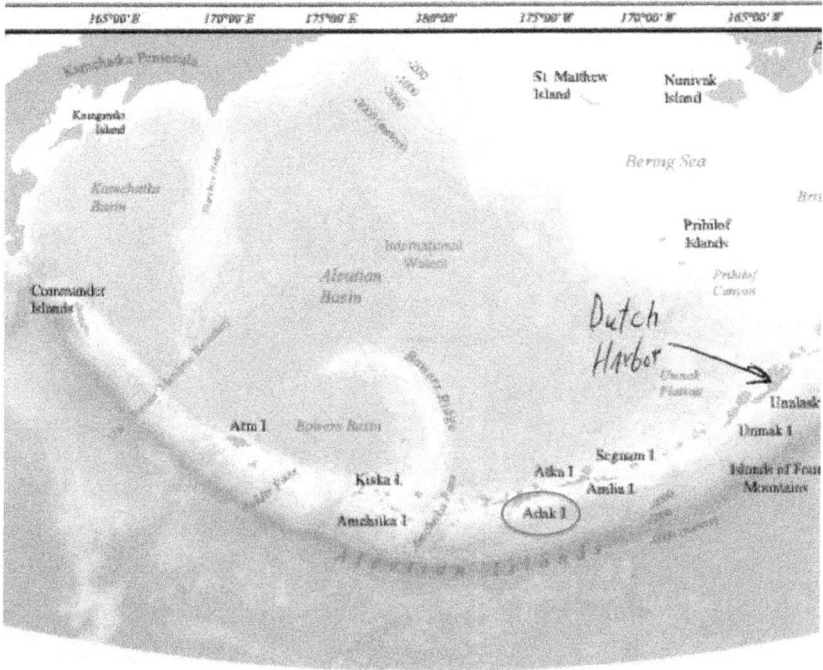

Western Aleutian Islands

From Adak, we turned around and went back up the Chain. Most of the islands had lava-like rock that rose steeply from the water's edge. They looked magnificent and forbidding. There were few trees, and I was surprised that any of the islands were capable of habitation.

Steaming for Kodiak, we stopped briefly to pick up several refrigerated containers of fish at Sand Point. Sand Point was at the end of the Alaska Peninsula and the starting point for the Aleutians. I didn't go ashore.

I did go ashore in Kodiak, but not to the bars in town. Instead, I used my lunch hour to climb a hillock -- maybe 1200 feet in elevation -- opposite our dock. From there I surveyed the surroundings. Kodiak looked like a natural deep-water port, on a large island of the same

13

name that had much more vegetation than the Aleutians. The small town was encircled by steep hillsides from which wooden buildings seemed barely to hang. Downtown was a half-mile from our dock so instead of walking there I decided to go back to the ship and work.

Leaving Kodiak
(photo taken with my Kodak Instamatic 110)

After Kodiak we steamed to Cordova. Cordova is a fishing town on a hillside at the mouth of the Copper River, nestled amongst spectacular mountains and glaciers at the southern end of Prince William Sound. Accessible only by sea and air -- there were no roads through the steep mountains -- it looked like a couple thousand souls called Cordova home. I decided to take a night off from painting and went ashore.

Approaching Cordova
(photo taken later with a better camera than mine)

Cordova had basically one main street with a drugstore, assorted shops, a couple of seedy hotels, and lots of bars. I chose an older-looking establishment, the Alaskan Hotel and Bar, and went inside for a beer. There was an old-timer to my right, drinking water, and as we got to talking it turned out he had grown up in Westport, Washington. He said he'd come north 20 years before to try to make his fortune fishing salmon.

He was semi-retired now -- not rich but comfortable -- and waxed nostalgic, giving me a bit of history. The town had once been a railhead of sorts. Kennecott Copper erected an elaborate 100-mile rail line to Cordova from its mines high up in the Copper River Valley. After laying claim to the richest mother lode of copper ever found -- during the Alaska Gold Rush at the turn of the century -- Kennecott pretty much owned this part of Alaska.

15

"There was so much ore coming out of the Wrangell Mountains that the tycoons who controlled Kennecott Copper bought the Alaska Steamship Company so they would own the ships that took the copper from Cordova down to Puget Sound to the smelter in Tacoma. I guess the fat cats weren't happy until they completed their monopoly. It was in 1908 that the railroad started, the same year that this hotel opened and the same year I was born."

Alaskan Hotel and Bar (many years later)

"I've heard of Alaska Steamship," I said while signaling the stocky barmaid for another beer. "That's the shipping line that cornered the

16

market for bringing freight up here. Why aren't any of their ships tied up here at the docks now?"

"They're almost belly-up. I don't think they can compete with your outfit, Sea-Land. Plus, the state started its own ferry system 10 years ago. That cut into Alaska Steamship's passengers as well as its freight revenue."

"Do the Kennecott people still own Alaska Steamship?"

"No. The copper ran out in 1938 and the railroad was abandoned. Kennecott sold off Alaska Steamship, too."

'Rape and split,' I thought. I thanked the old-timer for his history lesson, drained my beer, and went back to my ship. From Cordova we went back to Kodiak, then to the Aleutians again.

In Prince William Sound
(taken with a borrowed camera many years later)

III

On October 10th we were in the middle of the Chain when news came over the radio that Spiro Agnew had resigned. Agnew was Richard Nixon's Vice-President and widely hated by many for his proclamation that the "silent majority" approved of all the crap that he and "Tricky Dick" were doing. Agnew pled 'no contest' to the bribery and corruption charges brought against him. Nixon-haters were ecstatic. (Little did we know that Nixon himself would resign the following August.) The young guys in the crew announced a party.

The 'Spiro Agnew Good-bye Party' was held in Pat's and my fo'c'sle. The small space was jammed. One of the Ordinaries brought a tape player and I heard Stevie Winwood and Traffic singing "The Low Spark of High-Heeled Boys" for the first time. Some marijuana got passed around. Everybody had a good time.

Drugs in the merchant marine were a big no-no long before Nancy Reagan started her 'just say no' campaign. I guessed that the strict penalties were designed to discourage smuggling. A merchant seaman can murder his own mother and still go to sea. But if caught with a single joint it means the loss of seaman's papers possibly for life.

The S.S. Summit put into Cordova in the morning of October 18th, eight days after the party. After I blew tubes the First ordered me and Pat to go forward and grease the Manitowoc crane.

"This is bullshit," Pat said as we stood near the bow. "This crane doesn't need to be greased. Something's going on . . ."

Just as he said that, one of the Third Mates walked up and demanded that we walk aft with him.

The Third Mate took us to the Captain's office and told us that the Captain had given a direct order that we were to wait there. The Third

Mate stood next to us like a prison guard. I wondered what it was all about.

After about 10 minutes the Mate's walkie-talkie crackled with instructions that we were to be escorted to our fo'c'sle. The Mate took us down several decks to the quarters for unlicensed seamen. Once we got to our fo'c'sle, so many people were waiting for us in the small space that, after we went in, there was no room for the Third Mate. The Cordova Chief of Police identified himself and his Sergeant, James Estes. The Sergeant was kind of fat and I later learned that he was called "Tubby." Also there, observing, were Chief Kruger and Mr. Wright, the Chief Mate. He was from Seattle. I'd not yet met Mr. Wright but had already heard about him from the Ordinaries. He was said to be a fair man, unlike a lot of bully-boy Chief Mates who let power go to their heads.

McKinley, the Chief of Police, ordered Pat to open the combination lock hanging on the latch to his locker. After Pat opened his locker, the Sergeant searched it. Tubby Estes found a King Edward cigar box. Inside were a lot of marijuana seeds and stems, and some rolling papers, but no actual 'leaf' to smoke. The Sergeant handed the cigar box to Chief McKinley. "You're under arrest," the Chief said to Pat. After reading Pat his Miranda rights, he directed the Sergeant to take Pat away.

It was my turn next. I opened my locker. Chief McKinley acted increasingly frustrated when he couldn't find any drugs or paraphernalia. He finally gave up, and it looked like I was to be spared arrest. Chief Kruger left at that point, apparently satisfied he still had at least one Wiper, but the Chief Mate and the Chief of Police remained.

The Summit was port-side-to the dock and part of the gangway was just outside my fo'c'sle. Through the porthole, I watched Tubby Estes march Pat down the gangway to a waiting squad car. 'Pat's a good worker,' I thought. 'Even though this is only his second ship, he's a natural. If he gets convicted for marijuana possession, he'll never go to sea again.' I looked around. Mr. Wright looked uncomfortable and was staring at his shoes. Police Chief McKinley was standing with his right elbow propped on my bunk -- the top one -- and seemed to be daydreaming. On the bed next to his elbow was the cigar box, with all the evidence against Pat.

Meanwhile I had been standing at the other end of the bunkbeds in front of the two lockers. Seeing my chance I calmly walked toward Chief McKinley, reached up, and grabbed the cigar box. Moving quickly, I stuck my arm through the porthole and dropped the cigar box into Prince William Sound.

Chief McKinley did a double-take like a cartoon character, his eyes darting back and forth between the top bunk and the porthole. When it sunk in that his box of evidence was now jetsam, he turned to me with daggers in his eyes. I shrugged and said, "Just trying to help a shipmate." His face turned beet-red and he lunged at me. I squared off to fight, my back to the lockers.

Chief McKinley was older and maybe an inch shorter than me but he was twice as wide. I didn't have a chance against him even if he didn't have a gun, which he did. Perhaps realizing that the Chief Mate was watching, McKinley stopped when his face was an inch from mine. "I'm going to make your life miserable, boy!" He almost spat the words but kept his voice low enough that the Chief Mate couldn't hear them.

This is not the Cordova jail in 1973 but it looks like it

Chief McKinley made good on his promise. I was arrested and taken to jail with Pat, charged with Possession of Marijuana. I was prepared for charges of Destruction of Evidence or Obstruction of Justice -- for both of which I was guilty -- but Chief McKinley was threatening my livelihood. Tubby Estes swore out a Criminal Complaint in front of a judge, falsely stating that he found marijuana in my possession. Before we were taken to jail, Pat and I were marched up to the Captain's office at separate times and presented with a description of our misdeeds that was recorded in the ship's Log Book.

Pat refused to sign, protesting that the search was illegal. I did sign, even though there were no "vials" of marijuana in Pat's locker. Stems were just as illegal and I figured that the description of the warrantless search was accurate. Anyway, all I was admitting to by signing was that the log book entry had been read to me. Chief Kruger and Mr.

Wright were both honest men and I'm sure they understood what a "vial" is. I'm not so sure why they signed off for the log book entry. I know they faced heavy pressure from the Captain. Marijuana stems carried the same criminal consequences as marijuana 'vials'. Perhaps they were thinking: 'Why quibble?'

SS Summit   Official Number 243658

Extract of Official Log Book Entry

Dated: 10-18-73

Upon docking at the Port of Cordova, the Cordova Chief of Police and his Sergeant met the ship and came aboard immediately. They were escorted by the Chief Mate and the Chief Engineer to wipers' foc'sle and conducted a search for marijuana. Evidence of marijuana was found in an ashtray in the room. A further search was conducted and upon finding a locker with a lock on it the Wiper, Patrick Hynes, who owned the locker was sent for. Upon entering the room, Hynes opened the locker. The Chief of Police looked through the locker and at about the same time, Hynes, the wiper, said, "I'll show you what you're looking for", or words to that effect. He then produced a cigar box containing at least two vials of marijuana. The Wiper, Hynes, was removed from the room. The other Wiper, John W. Merriam, remained in the room. Later, in the presence of the Chief of Police and the Chief Mate, the Wiper, Merriam, threw the cigar box out the port hole and said, "just trying to help a buddy", or words to that effect.

Donald R Foster   17216 147¾ SE
Donald R. Foster, Master - SS Summit BK-034644
                                               Renton 98055

Elmer W. Kruger   803 Camino Amigo
Elmer W. Kruger, Chief Engineer - SS Summit Z-28083   Danville, ~~Wash~~ Calif.

James R. Wright   5263 Forest Ave SE
James R. Wright, Chief Mate - SS Summit Z-1165466   Mercer Isl.

The above Entry has been read in my presence and/or been read by me

REFUSED TO SIGN   *John Merriam*
Patrick R. Hynes Z-538-54-4795   John W. Merriam Z-534-56-2121

My copy, after I got logged and taken to jail

22

The Cordova jail was a Quonset hut left over from World War II. Pat and I were in the same cell but, convinced the cell was bugged, we didn't talk much. "Think about the Tremolos," I said to Pat as the jail door was locked behind us. I used rock'n'roll code to reference "Silence is Golden," the hit by a British group.

Pat also thought the search of our fo'c'sle was illegal because the cops didn't have a warrant. We weren't offered a phone call and even if we had been we didn't know who to call. 'I'd have to be a lawyer myself,' I thought bitterly, 'to get out of here.'

This is the first of my souvenirs from Cordova

Bail was set at $500, each. Pat and I both had more than $500 coming to us in wages but we had to get it from the Captain. The SIU contract has a provision that seamen can demand a draw on their wages at least once every five days when a vessel is in port. The Captain put out a draw in Kodiak, less than five days before, so he didn't have to give us another draw on our wages unless he wanted to. That meant we couldn't make bail unless the Captain was willing to give it to us.

The Captain gave me a chance to beg for my freedom. At about 2100 hours, 12 hours after I was thrown in jail, a different deputy escorted me back to the ship and took me to the Captain's office. I'd only seen him a couple of times before and never talked with him. Captain Foster was an emaciated-looking man who I guessed to be in his early 50s. He sat opposite me in his office chair, his legs crossed, and held a short glass containing a light-brown liquid. I smelled Scotch whisky.

"That was a pretty stupid stunt you pulled this morning, Wiper."

"I was just trying to help out a friend, sir."

"What would you say if I told you that your 'friend', along with two Ordinaries, is supplying drugs to the entire Aleutian Chain?"

I didn't say anything even though I knew it wasn't true. What I knew was no match for the Captain's alcohol-fueled paranoia.

The captain then gave me a lecture on the evils of marijuana. "You're new on here. I'm going to give you a break." I heard the clink of ice cubes as the Captain swirled his glass. "I'll allow you a $500 draw." I groveled with gratitude.

I bailed out of jail and rejoined the ship. Pat wasn't so lucky. The only way he could get his wages to post bail was to quit, which is what he did. That was exactly what the Captain wanted. Unfortunately for

Pat, I heard through the grapevine that the cigar box floated and was retrieved by the Cordova Harbormaster. I also heard that Pat beat the Possession charge. But if the cigar box floated and if the search was legal, I didn't know how he beat it. The pressure was on the two Ordinaries who were friends of Pat, and they soon quit also.

The new Bull Wiper

IV

I stayed on the S.S. Summit. As the only one remaining from Pat's group of friends, all eyes were on me. A condition of my bail was that I stay in Alaska. That would put me in technical violation every time I rode the Summit to Seattle. I was nervous that a single phone call could get me in a lot of trouble if someone squealed about me leaving Alaskan waters. It was time to compromise. When we were in Kodiak I skipped lunch, walked to a barbershop, and got about half my hair whacked off -- it was now above my shoulders but still lower than my ears. I tried to straddle the political fence that separated young people at the time. I also started going to bars with my shipmates, trying to fit in.

A new Wiper came aboard. Chuck was in his 40s but had no teeth and looked 20 years older. He hailed from the Ballard district in Seattle and was a professional Wiper, seemingly without ambition to do anything else. We got along well. Chuck liked his beer -- bragging that he'd "quit drinking" (hard liquor) several years before -- and downed a six-pack or two every evening after he knocked off work. Pat's forced departure meant that I was now the Bull Wiper so Chuck had to blow tubes. I still did it occasionally to help out, in deference to Chuck's age, especially on mornings after he'd had two six-packs instead of one. In the evenings, we both continued Pat's project of color-coding all the lines for the various systems in the engine room.

I also took over from Pat in helping the Chief Engineer. Elmer Kruger was a kindly man in his 50s. He showed me how to charge and maintain the reefer units for the refrigerated containers on deck. The Chief said he was training me to do his job so he wouldn't have to do it. I was happy to learn.

John the Electrician (facing rail) and Chief Kruger

I was making money hand-over-fist. As Bull Wiper, I helped take
on bunkers (fuel oil) and fresh water in Kodiak, tasks often undertaken
in the middle of the night. Along with repair jobs the Engineers didn't
want, I was putting in long hours and recording even longer ones on my
overtime sheet. There was a small "penalty" rate of overtime for
working long or odd hours and for doing particularly nasty work, like
going into the bilge. Once, to my embarrassment, I realized that I'd put
in for 28 hours of overtime in a 24-hour period. Before taxes, I was
making $1500-1700 a month! That was far more than any of the Oilers
and Firemen who had a higher rate of wages but only worked eight
hours a day standing watches.

The weather that winter started out unusually mild. The Japanese
Current mollifies Alaskan weather extremes near the ocean and it rarely
gets below freezing. There was one afternoon in early December, as
we steamed up the Aleutian Chain, when the thermometer hit the upper
60s Fahrenheit. I was helping Chief Kruger weld an 'eye' onto a hatch

cover at the time so the hatch cover could be lifted by the gantry and gave serious consideration to taking off my shirt and sunbathing on deck. It soon got colder and the dark nights lasted for all but five of the 24 hours in a day.

The Pavlov volcano in the Aleutians blew its top off on December 12th. We were close but not close enough to see any shooting flames or lava. An earthquake accompanied the eruption, I was told, but if there was any wave action, called a tsunami, I never felt it.

The Engineers, like other officers, crew, and even the Captain, didn't last long and there was a constant turnover: some quit and others got fired; some got injured and others flipped out. Chief Kruger had a permanent job, rotating four months of work with two months of vacation. He got off for his vacation in the middle of December, just after Mt. Pavlov blew. I don't remember much about the relief Chief other than that he came from Minnesota and weighed better than 300 pounds. I heard him brag about suing Sears Roebuck after an aluminum ladder buckled under his weight. With the new Chief signing our OT sheets, Chuck and I had to work longer after supper, until 2130. We started at 1800 instead of 1730 hours, worked at a relaxed pace and took more smoke breaks. Color-coding of lines in the engine room progressed at about the same speed as before.

The weather turned nasty right after Chief Kruger left on vacation. The tall stacks of containers formed a sail of sorts, making it difficult to fight the wind. Some of the storms were so vicious that the S.S. Summit had to duck into coves and bays for hours, sometimes days, to seek shelter. Hiding from the weather so frequently meant there was no way to keep to any semblance of a schedule, and it greatly extended the days required for round-trips up and down the Aleutians.

It was during one such storm that the Summit hid for a few days just before Christmas off the island of Unalaska in Captain's Bay. We hadn't been to Adak for quite a while and some of the crew was running out of booze. The situation became a crisis when the Chief Cook ran out. The Chief Cook put out tasty meals but he was a stone alcoholic and couldn't function without blended whiskey. Those in the unlicensed crew who still had a stash of alcohol didn't offer any to the Chief Cook. I'd learned on other ships that boozers won't share when their supply is low. The only liquor for sale within hundreds of miles in any direction was in the town of Unalaska, next to Dutch Harbor on the same island, some three miles away over a low mountain pass on a snow-covered road. No vehicles were available. I volunteered to 'Save Our Ship' by walking to town.

I started out after supper and got to the store just before it closed at 1900. A half-gallon of Canadian Mist was available at a hugely-inflated price. I didn't quibble.

'It's Christmas Eve,' I thought. 'I should have a drink before I walk back.' Unalaska was a dreary little fishing village of wooden hovels. One of those hovels, close to the store, was the Elbow Room, the only bar between the Alaskan mainland and Adak. I went inside.

The Elbow Room was a simple, framed rectangle on the outside but warm and rustic inside. The bar was lined with fishermen acting more rowdy than the Marines on Adak. I ordered a double Jack Daniels, black label, and went to a table. If I sat at the bar, I probably would have been challenged to a fight. In seamen machismo, the size of one's vessel establishes a pecking-order of sorts. The Summit was far bigger than any fishing boat and I wasn't going to lie about where I came from. The boys at the bar were drunk enough that the mere length of my ship might be felt to put their manhood in question.

I was savoring my Jack Daniels when a large native woman sat down next to me on the settee against the wall. The Aleut squaw made small talk and scooted closer. The half-gallon of Canadian Mist between us was the only reason she couldn't snuggle right up next to me. I guessed her to weigh in at 240 pounds. I drained my glass and left quickly.

I was a quarter-mile away, on my snowy return to the ship, before I realized that I'd left the jug of Canadian Mist on the settee at the Elbow Room. I calculated the odds of the jug still being where I left it . . . and kept walking to Captain's Bay.

The crew of the Summit was in foul humor as we ate cold food until the ship fetched Adak.

The gas crisis started shortly after Spiro Agnew resigned, and the price of oil quadrupled. A lot of ships had to lay up due to the lack of fuel. The contract with the Navy meant the Summit never had a problem but, after one visit just before Thanksgiving, we didn't go to Seattle again for the rest of the time I had that job. That was bad for homesickness but good for staying in compliance with the conditions of my bail.

I was already worried about being a bail jumper after our one trip to Seattle. We returned to Alaska after the Thanksgiving weekend, and our first port was Cordova. My paranoia was running wild. I saw cops hiding behind containers on the dock and assumed they were waiting for me to come down the gangway. Afraid to leave the ship, I persuaded the Second-Cook-and-Baker to go to the courthouse in Cordova to see if there was a warrant outstanding for my arrest. The

Baker was a large man in his late 50s with salt'n'pepper hair. He reported back that there was no arrest warrant for me and I breathed a little easier. The Baker also told me that my trial date had been postponed to January 22nd.

My trial on the Possession charge had originally been scheduled for December. If I had quit the ship to go to court, I wouldn't have gotten in the 90 days' seatime I needed that year to keep my union seniority. I'd written a letter to the judge asking that my trial be delayed until January 22nd, when I calculated the Summit would be at or close to Cordova. Luckily, the judge had granted my request. I wrote that I needed more time to get a lawyer. Technically, that was true. Actually, I didn't think I needed to pay a lawyer big bucks to help me beat the criminal charge because I'd gotten the home addresses of Chief Kruger and the Chief Mate, Mr. Wright. I figured their testimony alone would get me off the Possession charge. But I wanted more than just to win the criminal trial. I wanted to sue the Captain, Tubby Estes, and the Chief of Police for false arrest. That was the real reason I wanted a lawyer.

Getting a lawyer wasn't easy. Telephone connections in the Aleutians were dicey, and I was almost never close to a telephone during business hours. Under the SIU contract, we could take one day off every month or receive an extra day's pay if we didn't. I took a half-day off in Kodiak not long after Pavlov erupted, got a fistful of change and went to a warm restaurant that had a pay phone.

My first call was to the American Civil Liberties Union in Anchorage to ask if they'd be interested in my case. I'd gotten college credit for volunteering at the ACLU office in Seattle and I knew the organization was interested in situations involving illegal search and seizure. The volunteer who answered the phone in Anchorage said the

31

ACLU directors were out of town so there could be no quick decision on my request. I then asked for a referral to a lawyer who was good with this kind of case. The young woman gave me the phone number of Stanley Cornelius. She said that he was working on an ACLU case, representing bottomless dancers for false arrest, based on their right to freedom of expression.

I lucked out and caught Mr. Cornelius in his office the first time I called. After I briefly explained my situation, he told me to send him a $500 retainer and a letter with more details. I agreed, ended the pricey phone call, and walked back to the Sea-Land dock.

I learned that, although my trial was to be in Cordova, my lawyer, the judge, and prosecutor were all based in Anchorage, a short 150-mile airplane ride away. Mr. Cornelius told me to come to Anchorage a few days before the trial date.

Other than one day per month, the SIU contract had no provision for taking time off. Even if a seaman got sick and needed only a couple of days to recuperate, the department head was supposed to call the hiring hall for a replacement. By January, I decided that I wanted to stay on the Summit for another 90 days if I could. I was making good money, even with the relief Chief using a lot of red ink on my overtime sheet, and Mr. Kruger was due back in a month. If I got in my 90 days for 1974 I wouldn't have to ship out again for a year and-a-half, until the last three months of 1975 if my money lasted. I asked the relief Chief to not call the SIU hall for the seven days I expected to be off the ship. Even though we had our differences, the relief Chief knew I was a hard worker to the point that he'd had to stop me from doing repairs by myself -- repairs that were supposed to be performed only by Engineers. He also knew that it was a crap-shoot about who would get sent to replace me. He agreed not to call the hall, on the condition that

I rejoin the Summit after no more than seven days. I was discharged from the ship in Adak.

Serial No. I 8412415	DEPARTMENT OF TRANSPORTATION UNITED STATES COAST GUARD Certificate of Discharge to Merchant Seaman

DEPARTMENT OF TRANSPORTATION
UNITED STATES COAST GUARD
Certificate of Discharge
to Merchant Seaman

Serial No. I 8412415

(Signature of Seaman)

R. P. Karluik
(Master of Vessel)

I HEREBY CERTIFY that the above entries were made by me and are correct and that the signatures hereto were witnessed by me.

Dated this 16th day of JANUARY 19 74

R. P. Karluik
United States Shipping Commissioner
(or Master of Vessel)

Note—Whenever a master performs the duties of the shipping commissioner under this act, the master shall sign the certification on the line designated for the shipping commissioner's signature.

534-56-2121

Name of Seaman John Wheeler Merriam
(In full)

Citizenship USA — U. S. Merchant Mariners Document No. z 534562121

Rating Wiper
(Capacity in which employed)

Date of Shipment 9-26-73

Place of Shipment Seattle, WA

Date of Discharge 1-16-74

Place of Discharge ADAK, ALASKA

Name of Ship SS Summit

Name of Employer Sea Land Service, Inc.

Official No. 243658 Class of Vessel Steam
(Steam, Motor, Sail or Barge)

Nature of Voyage Coastwise
(Foreign, Intercoastal or Coastwise)

Off to court!

V

On January 16th I got off the Summit and flew to Anchorage to meet my lawyer. Stan Cornelius struck me as slick but not overly energetic. He wore a wrinkled blue suit. Mr. Cornelius said the case against me was so weak that the prosecutor would likely try to make a deal.

I had fun in Anchorage, in between meetings with my lawyer, even though it was -15 degrees. (It got up to 0 during the short days.) With one high-rise building, Anchorage was the closest thing Alaska had to a city. I stayed in a downtown motel and spent my evenings at Chilkoot Charlie's or in Indian bars, seeking female companionship.

Sure enough, just before it was time to fly to Cordova for trial, the prosecutor wanted to deal. I sat in Stan Cornelius' office. "He offered to reduce the charge to Disorderly Conduct with a $25 fine if you'll plead guilty," Stan told me.

"No way!" I responded.

Stan picked up the phone and dialed. After some discussion with the prosecutor, he hung up and said: "The prosecutor will drop charges outright if you'll sign an agreement to not sue the Cordova Police."

I had to give this proposal some consideration. It would be great to have this whole business over with. 'On the other hand,' I thought, 'this trip has cost me $400 on top of about $300 in lost wages and the $500 I paid for lawyer fees. And what about Tubby Estes lying under oath to try to destroy my livelihood, to say nothing of what happened to Pat . . . ?!' After thinking for about 30 seconds, I said, "No deal!"

Stan called the prosecutor again. "He threatened to add charges for Destruction of Evidence and Obstruction of Justice if you won't make a deal," Stan turned to me after he hung up.

"That's what I should have been charged with in the first place!" I responded secretly rejoicing while thinking, 'That means they couldn't use the evidence against Pat. Maybe the seeds and stems bounced out of the cigar box when it hit the water. . .?'

"Right. They're fucking with you. Come to my office tomorrow."

The next day, January 21st, Stan told me that the prosecutor "got sick" and the judge couldn't make it to Cordova for at least a week. "The prosecutor proposed a two-week continuance."

"I can't wait that long!" Not only did I need to rejoin my ship, I'd been having a lot of fun in Anchorage and had spent most of the money I'd brought with me. I couldn't afford to stay on land in Alaska for two more weeks.

"When could you go to Cordova for trial?"

"How about early April?" I said after thinking for a moment. If I stayed on the Summit until April 5th I'd have my 90 days for that year, too. By then I'd be rich!

"I'll see what I can do," Stan said.

I stuck with my original plane reservations and flew to Cordova on January 22nd. With no trial to attend, I killed time by walking on the docks and around town, then checked in to the Alaskan Hotel and Bar and got a cheap room upstairs. I read in the newspaper that the Anchorage Police voted to join the Teamsters' Union. Although the agreement didn't affect the tiny Cordova Police Department, I wondered if Chief McKinley and Tubby Estes would have treated me any better if we were union brothers. Lucky for me, I didn't run into either one of those guys. I didn't see the old fisherman I'd talked to, either.

Also lucky for me, the S.S. Summit was close to her schedule and I rejoined her the day after I arrived in Cordova.

If I thought the weather had been bad before, I hadn't seen a thing. In early February the shit hit the fan. Winds of better than 100 knots made steerage impossible and the S.S. Summit basically had to hide wherever she could. The radar got blown off. Even if we could control our heading, we wouldn't know where we were going. There was one time when we couldn't put into port for six days.

The times we did try to make port often meant we had to change course and be in the trough -- broadside to the seas -- and take some 40-degree rolls. Unless you're a mountain climber or expert downhill skier, it's not possible to remain upright at 40 degrees without holding onto something really tight. I was young and stupid, had no problems, and thought it was all good sport. I jumped around and walked up the bulkheads as the ship lay over as far as an English motorcycle taking a high-speed corner. Those who were older, fatter, or in worse physical condition had a lot of problems, however, and there were many injuries. One of the Oilers broke his shoulder.

One of the 40-degree rolls caused the 60-ton Manitowoc crane on the bow to break loose from its chain binders and fall over. The next roll pushed part of the crane through the rail on the forward main deck. One of the treads hung precariously over the starboard side. I had nightmares about the Summit capsizing. Those nightmares were given more fuel from an incident earlier that winter that I'd read about in the Kodiak newspaper. A foreign-flag tanker went down during a storm off the Queen Charlotte Islands of Canada not far from the border with Alaska. According to the newspaper, a lifeboat from the ship was recovered close to where the tanker sank. The lifeboat was perfectly dry inside, and no one was in it.

I'm not sure how the crane got righted and put back into position. I was working below the next time we put into Kodiak. The deck department must have found some way to rig the downed ship's crane to the huge shoreside crane.

High winds and freezing temperatures caused the spray to freeze. For a couple of days during the worst of that combination, four inches of solid ice coated every surface on the Summit. She looked like a ghost ship. This was more fun and games for me. For kicks I'd shoot 30 feet across the fantail on ice at the back of the ship -- setting a speed record for travel between the house and the rail without skates -- to dump garbage into the North Pacific. It was not fun and games for fishing boats, however. The smaller vessels sometimes got top-heavy with ice on their crab pots, rolled over, and sank. The ice formed so quickly that those in the crew, using axes, couldn't chop it off fast enough. I heard in a Kodiak bar that something like 17 fishing boats went down that winter -- some with all hands lost -- the worst year on record.

SIU seamen in the Seattle hiring hall, even B-books, knew better than to join the Summit at that time of year, and replacements started arriving from San Francisco and New York instead.

By January 23rd, when I rejoined the Summit in Cordova, I'd been on her longer than anyone except the Bo's'n and a couple of the cooks. It was also the longest I'd ever held a job. Chuck and I got into an argument over who was the Bull Wiper. Even though I'd been on the ship longer, my most recent Coast Guard Certificate of Discharge had me leaving the vessel on January 16th. We compromised and each blew tubes every other week.

A new First Ass't Engineer came aboard in early February. He was a couple years older than I was, about the same size but a little heavier, and had short black hair that was slicked down with Brylcream. I can't remember his real name; I called him Party Boy. He often had liquor on his breath and didn't work overtime. He'd gone to the Merchant Marine Academy at King's Point, New York, but he didn't like to work and I wondered how he'd gotten his First Assistant's license at such a young age.

One afternoon I was walking from the machine shop to the main engine room. Party Boy was sitting in the fireroom bullshitting with the 12-4 fireman. As I walked past the chair in front of the furnaces, Party Boy stuck his foot out to trip me. I kicked his foot away, hard, with my steel-toed boot. He sprang upright and we started grappling. I put him in a headlock and asked if he wanted me to twist his neck. "Mmpldufllk . . .!" Party Boy's mouth was pushed into my oil-stained T-shirt. I let him go.

The new First and I maintained something like an armed truce after that episode. I did repair jobs that he should have done, and he backed me up with the relief Chief, so I could write almost anything I wanted on my OT sheet.

In the middle of February, we tied up to the dock at Cordova around suppertime. At 1800 I stood in the shaft alley wondering what to paint next. Chuck was on a ladder, high up in the main engine room, finishing our most recent color-coding project while the Summit wasn't rolling so violently. The propeller shaft can only be painted in port, when it turns very slowly -- about one rotation per minute -- for the purpose of maintaining lubrication to moving metal parts. Pat hadn't mentioned the correct color for the shaft and none of the Engineers seemed to know. I was toying with the idea of changing it from generic white to a psychedelic paint job when I felt someone's presence. It was Party Boy, making a rare after-supper appearance in the engine room.

"The police just came aboard with an arrest warrant. I was sent to find you."

"Thanks, First." I bolted past him to the ladders and left the engine room like I'd been shot from a cannon.

The Summit had tunnels underneath the main deck, running the length of the ship next to the hull on either side. I ran up the starboard tunnel to the bow, popped up to the main deck, and then disappeared among the containers in #1 hold.

It was cold in #1 hold. While probing for sources of heat from steam lines, I wondered why my $500 bail hadn't simply been transferred to the new charges. I never found out. I didn't have to hide long enough to worry about hypothermia. About four hours later the ship cast off and we steamed for Kodiak. I don't know who was looking for me but I never heard a single footstep in pursuit. From later scuttlebutt I learned that the new Captain had ordered all hands to help the Cordova Police search the ship. The unlicensed crew refused, unless they were paid overtime. The only officers who joined the search were a couple of suck-up Third Mates and one Third Engineer. I also found out what the new charges were. The prosecutor made good on his threat and charged me with Destruction of Evidence.

My trial got continued until the second week in April. Chief Kruger came back in late February, and it wasn't long before Party Boy got fired. I laid low every time we put into Cordova but no more police came aboard. Chuck and I finished color-coding every line in the engine room and went on to other painting projects.

The First Assistant who replaced Party Boy was a wizened old fart marking time until he retired. He didn't like it that I ran around the engine room like I owned the place. In early April, not long before I was to quit the Summit to go to trial, he announced that I was to take my day off when we were in Cordova, whether I liked it or not. The SIU contract didn't really say that seamen had the option of not taking off one day per month and Chief Kruger was enough of a politician that he wouldn't countermand his First Assistant Engineer to protect a Wiper. Since I wasn't getting paid for the day, my choice was between staying on the ship or taking my chances in Cordova. Ships are prisons of sorts, and after six months I was feeling like a prisoner. The jail cell in Cordova was actually bigger than my fo'c'sle. It was obvious. I needed to get off that ship regardless of peril.

I made arrangements with a few of my shipmates to post bail in case I got busted, and the next morning I slipped down the gangway at Cordova. I walked around, keeping a lookout for Tubby Estes and

Chief McKinley. From earlier visits, I knew that the Alaskan Hotel and Bar made a good sandwich and I decided to have an early lunch.

Oops!

I sat at the wooden bar next to one of the only patrons at that hour. We got to talking and he started bragging about his fishing boat, a 30-foot gillnetter tied up not far from the bar. I told him that if he took me out in his boat for the rest of the day, I'd work as his deckhand for free. "Buy me a jug," he replied, "and we'll go out as long as you like."

"OK, it's a deal!" We went to a liquor store next door where I bought a fifth of cheap vodka before we walked down to his boat.

I got a sight-seeing tour on magnificent Prince William Sound that afternoon. I didn't have to work because my host got too drunk to do any fishing. He got so drunk, in fact, that I had to bring the boat back myself and tie her up. I left him, passed out in the cabin, and returned to my ship at dusk.

VI

On April 6th I quit the S.S. Summit in Kodiak. It felt like spring and I ditched all my heavy work clothes, leaving with just a jean jacket and wearing tennis shoes. I took a ferry to Homer, hitchhiked to Anchorage, checked into a cheap motel, and called my lawyer.

Leaving the Summit for good

As soon as the prosecutor heard that I was back in town and ready to go to trial he dropped all charges. I asked Stan Cornelius about suing the Cordova Police, Sea-Land, and the Captain for false arrest. Stan hemmed and hawed, said he was not familiar with maritime law and made an appointment for me to come in two days later.

With time on my hands, I went to the Coast Guard office and took examinations for the ratings of Oiler, Fireman, and Watertender. Between what Chief Kruger taught me and knowing all the auxiliary systems from color-coding the lines, taking those tests was like a walk in the park. The Coast Guard officer grading the exams said my scores were the highest he'd ever seen in Anchorage.

On April 15th I went to Stan Cornelius' office on K Street. Another guy was there, wearing a suit, who Stan introduced as his "partner" Ron West. Stan told me that he had to stop practicing law for a while and that Ron West would be taking over my case. Stan was short on details to explain this event. I got the impression that he was messing with some of the powers that be in Anchorage. West handed me a contingency fee agreement -- I only had to pay lawyer fees if my case was successful. I signed. The meeting ended on a gloomy note. 'Poor Stan,' I thought.

A plane ticket from Anchorage to Seattle cost a small fortune. I planned to work my way home on a fishing boat, saving my money to live on and maybe go back to school. Much of the fishing and crabbing in Alaska is done by boats based in Seattle, and I figured that getting a deckhand job would be no problem. After meeting with the lawyers I threw my pack over my shoulder, checked out of the motel, and walked to the waterfront.

There were no fishing boats! I soon learned that Anchorage was not a fishing port. 'What the hell,' I thought, 'I'll hitchhike home.' I asked about the road to Fairbanks and stuck out my thumb.

That was one of the stupidest choices I've ever made. It was 2500 miles to Seattle, 1500 of that on the unpaved Alcan Highway. Even though I thought it was spring, as soon as I got into the interior I saw that the rivers were still frozen solid. In April all the traffic was headed north, to Alaska, with none going south. I did a lot of walking, while cursing myself as a fool for not bringing a sleeping bag and heavier clothes. A raven started circling overhead. I worried that the raven knew more about my chances for survival than I did and was waiting

42

for me to stumble. The sun went down and it started getting very cold . . . But that's another story. Suffice it to say that I made it to Seattle after eight days.

With the money I saved in Alaska I rented a house, got a new girlfriend, and went back to the University of Washington for a few academic quarters.

Ron West didn't return my phone calls inquiring about progress in the case. Instead I got a bill for $66 for work on the criminal case that had been dismissed before I'd even retained him. I called again and someone in West's office told me that if I didn't pay the $66, I'd be turned over to a collection agency. I was not pleased with this turn of events. On the other hand, I was consumed by a desire for revenge against Captain Foster, to say nothing of Chief McKinley and Tubby Estes. And searching for another lawyer in Alaska was a daunting prospect. I paid the $66 that October.

After paying Ron West money he hadn't earned, I got more adamant about learning of developments in my case. I got through to him once -- perhaps by a fluke -- later that autumn. West told me he'd filed a lawsuit against Sea-Land and the Captain and said he'd send me a copy of the Complaint. That shut me up for a little while. I wasn't upset that the Cordova Police were not named in the lawsuit. Stan Cornelius didn't know maritime law but once told me that it would be tough to sue the cops, even if the search was illegal, because the Captain invited them aboard.

I never received a copy of the lawsuit. I made more phone calls to West, always in vain.

By April 1975 I got fed up with trying to communicate with him, my own lawyer, and bought a plane ticket to Anchorage.

I went to West's office on K Street and demanded my file. There was nothing to reflect that any lawsuit had been filed. I never got to see Mr. West in person.

From West's office I went to the Alaska State Bar Association and filed a complaint. I wrote that, in addition to shaking me down for $66, West lied to me about pursuing my case. I called him sloppy and a disgrace to the bar. The Bar Association seemed to take my complaint seriously.

From there I shopped my case around to any lawyer in Anchorage who would meet with me. I got three appointments. The first two lawyers wouldn't take my case on a contingent fee basis, as opposed to hourly fees. They said that the law of search and seizure aboard merchant ships fell into a gray area of the law, and they wouldn't risk not getting paid. The third lawyer seemed to know a little more about maritime law. "The Captain is god on a ship," he said. "He could have searched your locker any time he felt like it, with or without a warrant or probable cause. The same goes for Customs and Immigration. Local police need a warrant to search. The question is: Can the Captain delegate his authority to the local police and get around the requirement for a warrant? The answer is: probably not, and certainly not if the warrantless search results in criminal charges." He continued, thinking out loud: "But what if the Captain delegated to the local police only the authority he had to search and confiscate contraband, but not to bring criminal charges for possessing it?" The third lawyer didn't have an answer to his own rhetorical question, and told me my case was too uncertain to take on a contingent-fee basis.

It looked like I was out of luck in my quest for revenge.

It was my last night in Anchorage and I decided to splurge by having dinner at a fancy joint called The Restaurant. Inside, it looked remarkably similar to a Seattle restaurant called 13 Coins. The news at the time was full of stories about the fall of Saigon. The man in the stool-bucket-seat next to me at the bar had a newspaper up to his face. On the front page, facing me, was a large photograph of Gerald Ford kissing a Vietnamese baby who'd been flown off the roof of the U.S. Embassy by helicopter. It looked like two wars -- U.S. vs. Viet Nam and Wiper vs. Sea-Land & Cordova P.D. -- were both over at the same time. It was time to move on.

The Alaska Bar Association sustained my complaint against Ron West although I'm not sure what punishment was meted out, if any. West backed off the $66 as a mistake and initially denied having a contingent fee agreement with me. When confronted with the signed contingent fee agreement, he started whining about 'not having to sue when I don't think it justified'.

Three years later I was awarded a $10,000 union scholarship from the SIU. The scholarship was designed to pay for four years of college. By 1978, I'd been fooling around at the UW for so long that I had enough credits for a Bachelor's degree. It seemed silly to waste the scholarship on more undergraduate credits so I applied to a bunch of law schools. I petitioned the UW to graduate and petitioned the SIU to divide the scholarship into three years instead of four, for a law school curriculum. I was successful on both counts.

In 1978, $10,000 was enough money to pay law school tuition for all three years. I still needed money to live on and took a year off to go back to sea. I graduated in 1982, passed the bar examination, and have practiced maritime law ever since. My practice is now limited to the

45

representation of maritime claimants for wages or injury. I try to return phone calls the same day, tell no lies, and don't make promises I can't keep.

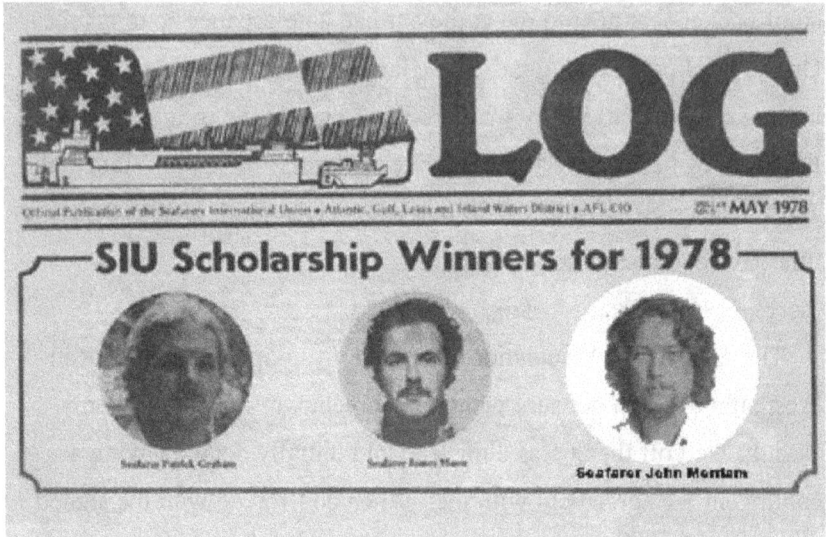

SIU newspaper

EPILOGUE

I found Pat again in early 2006, 32 years after I left him sitting in the Cordova jail. It turned out we had lived only a mile apart for 14 years, in the Northgate district of Seattle until I moved to a different neighborhood in 2003. I finally found out what happened to him.

"They moved my trial from Cordova to Anchorage. I don't know why." Pat now has short hair and has gained a little weight but he still looks trim. "I had $200 to last me a month until the trial date. My public defender didn't know anything about maritime law. Neither did the prosecutor. I kept yelling that there was no warrant and the search was illegal. When we went to court, the public defender told the prosecutor that the search was illegal. The prosecutor didn't know any better so he dropped the charges and I walked. After getting out of the Cordova jail, I never heard another thing about the cigar box."

Pat told me he now worked as a contractor, laying tile, and was happily married with three kids. After we got busted, he never went to sea again.